Pr

The Hidden Sentence™

Prison:
The Hidden Sentence™

WHAT TO DO WHEN YOUR LOVED ONE IS ARRESTED AND INCARCERATED

Julia Lazareck

ISBN: 978-1-7354388-0-1

To have compassion, you need to start with empathy.
In memory of my brother, who taught me both.

Contents

Acknowledgments   9

Introduction   11

CHAPTER ONE

Arrest   17

   Growing Up Together   17

   How It Started   20

   What We Didn't Know   23

CHAPTER TWO

Court   33

   The Trial   33

   The Verdict   36

   What We Didn't Know   39

CHAPTER THREE

Visitation   49

   Visit Preparation   49

   The Physical Visit   54

   What We Learned   59

CHAPTER FOUR

Stories   71

   My Brother Died In Prison   71

   Selected Stories   75

   Empathy   81

CHAPTER FIVE

Healthy You — A Call To Action   87

    Seeking Information   87

    Finding Support   92

    A Balanced Life   95

Conclusion   103

Next Steps   107

About the Author   109

Acknowledgments

First and foremost, I acknowledge my family for demonstrating strength in what they've been through in their lives so I had an example to follow.

I want to express my thanks:

> To my husband, Les, for listening, holding me, and being compassionate, even when he didn't understand me.

> To my friends who supported me and encouraged me to open up and share my story to release my hidden sentence so I could help others.

> To Adam Markel and his team from More Love Media, and Maura and Keith Leon and their team from YouSpeakIt Books, and Burnt Toast II Toastmasters Club, who heard my story and helped me provide this information to you.

Introduction

You get that call in the middle of the night. Your loved one says they are in jail, or it's a police officer on the other end of the line who tells you your loved one has been arrested.

Would you know what to do?

If you are going through the trauma of having a loved one taken into the prison system, I want you to gain the information you need, be prepared, and know you're not alone. There are millions of people in the United States going through this. Take care of yourself and obtain what you need to keep yourself healthy. Don't overextend yourself, either emotionally or financially.

You may not know someone in the prison system or you may not think you know someone who has had a loved one in the prison system—but chances are you talk to people every day who are in this situation, and they just don't mention it. When you do hear that someone has a loved one who has been incarcerated or taken into the prison system, this book will help you understand that folks on the outside are affected by incarceration, too. They did not commit the crime; however, people often look at them as if they committed the crime their loved one is charged with.

If you've never been through this process, there are so many things that you need to know to best support yourself and your loved one.

What will you do first when you receive the call?

This book will help you traverse the prison system from the time you receive that call to visiting your loved one who is in jail.

You will need to know:

- If you need an attorney
- What the rules are
- What applications you need to fill out
- How you can speak to your loved one
- What you should wear
- What you can bring

This book will walk you through the whole process from the time your loved one is arrested, to when they go to court, to visiting them — if, unfortunately, they are sentenced to prison.

Depending on the crime, there could be a stigma associated with your family.

You will wonder:

- How do you alleviate the stigma?
- How do you talk to people?
- How do you tell colleagues and employers?

- How do you tell friends?
- How do you deal with people who no longer want to be around you or your children?
- How do you keep a balanced life?

This book will answer those questions and more.

My name is Julia Lazareck. My brother, Bo, was convicted of a serious crime that I didn't talk about. I didn't tell anybody. I lived a hidden sentence, and I served the sentence with him. The only difference was that I was serving it on the outside. I served it alone. For fifteen years, I visited him. It was a financial and emotional burden on me.

Bo had alienated everybody. He was a loner and didn't have a lot of people in his circle, so I was his main contact with the outside world. I was the only person who visited him throughout the fifteen years of his incarceration.

I am writing this book to provide you with the information you need to navigate through the process. I don't want you to make the mistakes I made, to keep your feelings inside, to serve a hidden sentence like I did during the time my brother was incarcerated. Talking about the experience is freeing, and that is why I wrote this book. I want you to read others' stories so you can live a healthy life while your loved one is incarcerated.

For others, you can show compassion to families on the outside; support them and do not stigmatize them. Don't judge other people. Chances are you know someone dealing with an arrest in their family or in a situation where they are affected by incarceration or the prison system. This book will open your eyes so you know what to do and how to be compassionate to others.

I hope to help someone who has a loved one in the prison system. I also want to raise awareness and compassion in others who have not been through it so they can be prepared if it ever happens to their loved one.

Read the whole book. However, if you are currently experiencing something in particular, go to the chapter that reflects what you're going through. I hope reading it encourages you to share information, talk about it, and provide feedback to me, too. You can contact me at https://prisonthehiddensentence.com.

Chapter One

Arrest

GROWING UP TOGETHER

Life changes in a second. Something you've never imagined or even been aware of could happen to you. It doesn't matter who you are or where you come from, whether you're rich or poor, immigrant or born here. These things can happen to you. It's not only to people *over there* that these things happen, or to people you think are bad or deserving. Bad things happen to everybody.

I want you to understand where my brother and I came from and how shocking the arrest was. My hope is that sharing our story will better prepare you should you or someone you love end up in a similar situation. When you are aware of tools and resources ahead of time, you can better gather what you need in the moment and respond, even if you're experiencing trauma or stress. I want to share what my family was like before the arrest, and how our lives were changed.

Our Background

Our school bus stop was across the street so we didn't have too far to walk. *One . . . two . . . three . . . eighty-three*—it was eighty-three steps from my front door to the bus stop at the corner across from our home. It was a beautiful neighborhood, and in the fall, the trees would boast bright orange and yellow leaves.

When it rained or snowed, my dad would open the garage, and all the kids would run in and wait for the bus to arrive. The bus driver, Mrs. Harrison, would wait for us to gather our belongings and make our way toward the school bus. Other children were sitting there dripping wet from standing out in the rain, but our group had only a few drops from running the eighty-three steps to the bus. Dad would close the garage once we were safely on the bus.

We were a typical family back then: two parents, two children, and a dog. We didn't have a white picket fence, but we had parents who loved us. They provided a safe home and enough food to eat.

Note: Names and locations in this book have been changed to protect privacy.

We Were Close

My brother and I loved to climb the trees in our backyard when we were young. In the fall, we'd hide between the brilliant fall colors on the highest branches of the tree. When the leaves fell, my parents would give us rakes, and we'd make high piles of leaves. Yes, we'd jump in them. When the leaves fell, we knew winter was near, and it would soon be time for sledding.

We'd bundle up and drag our sleds down the street to the golf course and meet the other kids in the neighborhood. We'd sled for hours until we couldn't feel our noses or cheeks anymore. The walk home was chilling, and when we walked in the door, the heat would melt away any coldness left.

Every night, we'd have dinner together as soon as our father came home from work. Sundays were a family day, and my brother or I would get to ride with Dad to Red Moon Pizza to get the best tasting pizza I've had to this day. Afterward, we'd all jump in the station wagon and go to Carvel for ice cream.

We didn't know that our parents scrimped and saved to ensure we had a safe place to live, clothes on our backs, and food in our tummies. Whatever we didn't have, we didn't know that we didn't have it.

Living Together

As we grew into adulthood, I moved out of the house. It was tough for my brother. He did go to college, but he dropped out after two months. My dad couldn't understand that. Instead of going back home, my brother came and lived with me. I had an apartment with a friend he knew. The apartment had a large kitchen in it. We put a bed in the back of the kitchen so he could stay with us. It actually worked out well.

We all lived together about three years. Then, I moved out, and Bo kept the apartment for several more years. We continued to stay close and got together weekly.

When I bought my first house, he moved in with me. He was living with me for about a year. That is where this story started.

HOW IT STARTED

My brother became friends with Joe at work, and they would spend time together. Bo also became friends with Joe's wife, Renee, and her family. One day, Renee called and asked Bo about his visits to their home. Bo didn't know that the call was being recorded, and the police were trying to gather evidence about him. Even though he didn't agree to anything or incriminate himself, this phone call would be used as evidence against him.

After the call, he was shaken up. He said to me, "How could they say this? How could they say these things about me? I can't believe it." He was so hurt and so shocked.

Of course, I felt bad for him. I wanted to make things better, but of course I couldn't. I told him to relax, not to worry about it. They weren't his friends, and he could move on.

The Process

Several weeks after the call, he was arrested and asked to turn himself in, so he did. The bail was $5,000. In the big picture, we didn't imagine that anything would come of it. We bailed him out and he came home. He hired an attorney. Then people from the police department started coming to our house, asking to speak to me, to speak to my brother. The attorney told us not to talk to anybody, so we didn't. It was the unknowing that was the hardest at the time. It was the late 1990s, and there was no information available, no internet. We didn't know it was serious, or how serious it was. It was a time of not knowing, of living in fear of what was going to happen next, if anything was going to happen.

The Arrest

Because he was able to turn himself in, I was able to bring him in to the police station. We knew that the bail was $5,000, and we had to come up with 10 percent to pay the bail bondsman. I don't remember how, but we scraped the money together and had all the completed paperwork we needed from the bail bondsman to show the processing officer. I paid the bail and they processed him. Because we had all the paperwork, it took only a couple of hours for them to release him. At this point, we were still ignorant about the severity of the charges and the consequences. We thought because the bail was relatively low and the process was fast, it wasn't serious. We were ignorant, and we were fearful because we knew the next step was to go to court.

Entering the world of the prison system is like *entering another world,* one that you typically won't be aware of until you learn the rules.

From the very start, we had never seen or been around anything like this process or known anyone who has been in this kind of engagement with law enforcement or the criminal justice system.

Arrest Stories Shared by Others

My son was seventeen years old and living with a friend down the street. I was happy he was down the street, but I had no idea he had a drug problem. I would talk to him every couple of days. One day, his friend knocked on my door, crying, telling me my son had been arrested. I didn't know who to talk to or anything. I was able to see him in the detention center, but it was through a monitor. It was horrible. I couldn't believe I had a son in prison.

*

I never thought I'd be a mother with a son in prison. I found out my son was in trouble when I was watching the news. They showed his picture and said he had been arrested. I thought they were going to kill him.

*

My son was arrested, and I am the only one who went to see him in his prison. As a member of a law-abiding family, he was devastated. He was a husband and father to three other children and a serving police officer. He could already name the majority of the other prisoners in prison with him.

WHAT WE DIDN'T KNOW

When you are entering the prison system, it's like another world. My friend said it's like "pulling back the curtain on another universe." By knowing the rules and being prepared, you can better help your loved one.

We want to rehabilitate our loved ones if they do something criminal, and we want to protect our loved ones if they are innocent. My brother and I didn't know a lot, but we learned, too late. We don't want it to be too late for you.

Get an Attorney Right Away

An attorney is essential. My brother did hire one at first. I know of stories in which people hired attorneys they thought were good, but ended up not being good, and the attorneys did not have the loved ones' interests in their hearts and minds. You need to find the right attorney and secure one right away so your loved one doesn't incriminate themselves.

Most attorneys have a twenty-four-hour phone line, so if you do need one, chances are you can talk to somebody right away. You need to do your research too. It's pretty traumatic when this happens, when you get the call and find out somebody has been arrested. But you should check attorney websites. Search their names and see if there have been any cases they have won, if they have handled cases that are similar to yours. Check their fees. All the attorneys should be comparable. The first call should be free so you can obtain preliminary information and determine if you can afford an attorney.

However, if there is time, you might want to call more than one attorney. If you hire an attorney, you will need to provide a retainer. My brother went through several attorneys. If you end up hiring different ones, you want to make sure you put your money with the best defense. If you don't have the funds you need to hire an attorney, you can look into legal aid and call other support services that are available in your area. If you think that you will need a Public Defender, you can call their office to find out what the procedure is in your jurisdiction. If a Public Defender is needed, they are usually assigned at the first court hearing.

Should We Talk About It?

When the crime impacts another person or is about another person—especially a juvenile—you don't want to say anything that could be held against you or your loved one. It's not something you should talk to people about.

When this happens, who do you talk to? What do you do?

As mentioned above, it is important to secure an attorney and follow their directions. If you can't afford an attorney, you should still be mindful of who you talk to so you don't incriminate your loved one.

Kenisha's son was accused of stealing from a neighbor's garage. Kenisha wanted to apologize to the family, but was warned by her attorney not to. Her apology could have been construed as admitting to the crime and used in court against her son.

Who else do you tell?

We decided not to talk to anybody. When I say *we*, my brother would report back to only me. We didn't tell anybody what he was going through.

When these situations are reported on the news, the accused don't have the benefit of anonymity. Think of it. When you see that somebody on the news has been charged with committing a crime, you see their picture and you think they're guilty. It's not *innocent until proven guilty* anymore. Just remember that.

When you talk to people about your situation, they will have judgments and preconceived thoughts. It's really important you know who to talk to; you talk to safe people only. Take advice from your attorney and don't incriminate yourself or your family members.

Effects on Job and Family

When my brother told his employer he had to go to court, he was fired. He lost his finances and way of paying for his life. I lost a paying roommate because he had been paying rent and could no longer. I had to come up with the full house payment. That was only one of the ways it affected our family. Think of people who have children. If the breadwinner is taken into custody, who is going to pay the bills?

When you lose somebody who has been contributing to the household finances, there's more than a simple financial impact on the family. If it's a child, and you need to take time off, it affects your work. It's also an emotional burden.

It's like losing someone to the prison system when they are arrested. You don't know how long they will be in there. You don't know what's going to happen next. Just imagine the anxiety and stress you would feel along with the guilt and shame about a crime that affected other people.

Arrest Story of a Friend in Need

I was with a friend whose daughter was visiting her friend in college in another state. Her daughter was arrested for being drunk and disorderly. My friend was one of those overprotective mothers. She had never been in trouble—had never known anybody who had been in trouble with the police—and she was freaking out when her daughter called to tell her she had been arrested. Luckily, I was there and I was able to help her.

I had her call the jail to get the details.

When you call jail, ask as many questions as possible:

- What happened and what are the charges?

- What is going to happen next?

- Has a court date been set?

- How long will my loved one be in jail?

- When can they be released?

- Can they provide the names of local legal counsels?

- Can they provide the names of bail bondsmen in the area?

- How can money be put on my loved one's account?

- Can they have visitors (and you can ask what type of visits are available, such as through glass, video, or in person)? Where do the visits take place (address)?

- When will they see a medical professional if they have a medical condition?

- Are there applications you need to fill out or appointments to make if you want to visit?

Contact an attorney. I had her contact one right away. The attorney helped so much because he was local to the area, and he told her the process. If it had been needed, he could have provided a bail bonds company. In this case, she didn't need one. But if she had, she had that information.

If you do need to fill out any paperwork to visit, fill it out right away and find out what the process is.

If your loved one will be in jail for more than a day, ask if you can put money on their account so they can call you. Otherwise, they won't be able to contact you. Ask if you can put money on their account even if they are only there for a couple days.

Medical Needs

What if your loved one needs medication?

They will need to be seen by a medical professional who can provide an examination and prescribe medication. If your loved one takes medication for pain, diabetes, mental illness, or other conditions, call the facility to find out if they've seen a medical professional. Call again if necessary, until someone can verify that your loved one has seen a medical professional and can receive the medications they require.

Important Points

RECAP: Once you find out that your loved one has been arrested:

1. Call the jail and get as much information as possible. Inquire about medical care for any pre-existing conditions.

2. Call an attorney.

3. If bail is required, contact a bail bondsman; they can provide a lot of information.

4. Fill out any forms—for visitation, putting money on your loved one's account, or other needs.

5. Put money on account if your loved one is going to be there more than a day. They'll use this money for calls and possibly for personal items and vending snacks.

6. If required, schedule an appointment right away to visit.

Chapter Two

Court

THE TRIAL

A lot of us have seen courtrooms and trials on TV and been entertained by them. However, when you're there for a trial of somebody you love, it's a lot different. In this chapter, I wanted to share real-life situations in the courtroom so you know what it's like to watch a loved one go through the trial process and receive a verdict.

About a year passed between the arrest and the trial. During that time, my brother had a new job, and he moved into an apartment across the state. I didn't see him much until the trial. He transitioned from living with me, to being arrested, to moving out and getting his own place. He could not afford the attorney and was assigned a Public Defender.

This brings us to the trial almost a year later. The first day in court he pleaded not guilty and opted for a trial by jury. The trial took place the next day.

Being In the Courtroom

Being in the courtroom, on the day of the trial, was one of the scariest experiences I've had. The day of the trial, I met my parents at the courthouse. Even though we'd seen courtrooms on TV, it was so different from a television drama. We walked into the courtroom, and I sat with my parents on the hard wooden benches, a short pony wall separating us from the trial participants.

The family making the accusations against my brother sat across the aisle from us. On the left-hand side near the judge, the jurors were seated. There were two tables on the other side of the pony wall, facing the judge. One for the defense, where my brother and his public defender sat. My brother was sitting there, wearing a suit, waiting for the trial to begin.

The prosecutors were sitting at the other table. The judge sat in front of us on a raised platform in his chair with his gavel at hand. The court stenographer sat on one side and the bailiff stood nearby. It was surreal to be sitting there and seeing my loved one waiting to be prosecuted, not knowing what was going to happen.

The Plea Bargain

Before the trial started and again, before we had entered the courtroom, we did get to meet with my brother's attorney. He said the District Attorney (DA) was offering my brother five years to avoid going to trial. They didn't want to go to trial. They liked to work things out beforehand. A lot of times, when the court date arrives, the prosecutors will make a plea offer.

My brother said he did not commit the crime, and he wanted a trial.

During the plea bargain, the two parties went back and forth a few times. First, prosecutors offered him five years, and he wouldn't take it. Then the defense countered with six months and probation. My brother considered that, but the prosecutor wouldn't accept that. It almost seemed like the prosecutors wanted to go to trial. They offered the five years, and that was it. They did not negotiate any further during this plea bargain. It could've come out differently if they had.

My father took my brother aside and begged him to take the five-year plea, but he would not take it. My parents were so upset. When we walked into the courtroom, our hearts were low. The attorney had told us that if he was convicted, the minimum sentence would be life in prison.

It was horrible and icky sitting in the actual courtroom. Even though we were only my brother's family, the family making the accusations looked at us like *we* had done something criminal. It was just so awful—the jurors looked at us the same way.

We were the family. We were not the person being prosecuted. We were not the person accused of the crime. But we were sitting there. Because we were related, they looked at us with disgust. We felt horrible for many reasons: our loved one might be taken from us, we didn't know whether he had done it, and people looked at us and treated us like we were the criminals when we hadn't done anything.

The Actual Trial

The actual trial was agonizing. It only took a couple of hours. The attorney told us if the jury didn't deliberate long, the verdict might be in our favor. The jury came back and gave the verdict to the judge. We were hopeful. The attorney had given us hope because the jury did not deliberate long, the trial concluded quickly, and the testimony seemed in my brother's favor. He thought we might come out with a good verdict.

THE VERDICT

The bailiff brought the jury back into the courtroom, and they took their seats. The judge said a few things to the jury to make sure they were ready to give the verdict. Then the judge asked the jury foreman to read the verdict. This was the critical moment. They literally held my brother's life in their hands.

Before the jury foreman was asked to read the verdict, the judge asked my brother to stand. He stood up next to the public defender. I could see him shaking as the jury foreman started to read the verdict. I held my breath.

They found him guilty. As I mentioned earlier, the minimum sentence was life in prison. I couldn't even imagine how my brother felt at that point, or how anybody would feel if they were given life in prison. The sentence did not fit the crime.

The Shock

When the jury read their verdict, we were in disbelief. I went up to my brother, and I could feel the shock and anger in his eyes when I went to hug him. It was amazing that nobody stopped me. I was able to spend those couple of seconds with him before they took him away. I couldn't even imagine what was going through his mind. I needed some things from him. He was going away. I took his ring and his watch. I still have them to this day.

When I got back to my parents, I could see my dad. It was weird. He had the exact same look in his eyes as my brother—anger and shock and disbelief and fear. My mother was crying. They were losing their son.

Leaving the Courtroom

We didn't say much when we left the courtroom. When we left, life changed. Our lives would never be the same. My brother was gone—gone from us and taken into the prison system. My brother was still alive, but out of our reach, and there was nothing we can do to help him.

Stories

She was in the courthouse when he was sentenced. She couldn't believe that just anyone was allowed in the court hearings. On the left side were inmates handcuffed in their orange jumpsuits. Their family members were in the audience. They called the names, and the attorneys came up right then and there and talked to the judge. Her son took a plea deal.

She said, "My son took a plea deal. The judge asked him if there was anything he wanted to say. I don't really want to say exactly what he said, but he was sorry. He didn't want to go into the details, but he was sorry. The judge gave him his sentence. He changed the sentence from what the probation people had originally said. Right then and there, he was taken into custody."

*

It was an emotional process. I had to drive him to the courthouse, where he was sentenced seven to fifteen years. That drive was the hardest drive I ever had to take. It wasn't until two years later we found out that he didn't need to plea bargain for the charges because the attorney gave us ill advice. It was very hard on me to realize that I had driven to the court hearing where he was sentenced to find out later that the attorney I thought was going to help us didn't. It was a very trying time.

WHAT WE DIDN'T KNOW

It was such a traumatic experience for my family. The attorney could have helped us prepare better for this worst outcome. We didn't know what questions to ask. He could have told us that we wouldn't be able to see Bo before he was taken away by the bailiff, and he could have mentioned where they would take him. There were things that could have helped us get through the process a little easier.

There is no bandage; however, there are things we learned afterward that could have helped us. We didn't realize it at the time, but we had just become a *prison family*, a family who had received a sentence joining us to the prison system.

Preparing for Court

We were in shock because everything happened quickly, the speed of the trial and reaching a verdict. It's not like that for everybody. Sometimes, people go to court several times. It's not always that quick. This process could involve going to court only to have another court date scheduled. It could be weeks or months later. Your loved one could be sitting in jail, waiting for the next court date. Not everyone is released on bail or on their own recognizance. Depending on the crime and the circumstances, every case is different.

Part of the preparation for court is realizing it's different for everybody. You need to be prepared for your loved one to be taken away right then and there if a guilty verdict is reached. That could be the last time you see your loved one as a free person. Or if the trial isn't completed in that session, your loved one could be taken back into jail.

If your loved one was in jail or had to resume a trial after having been in jail, they are going to be handcuffed and in a jumpsuit when they come out. It is pretty hard seeing your loved one shackled. You can try to prepare yourself emotionally for what you're going to see and what you're going to hear. Be prepared for the worst outcomes, but hope for the best.

Talking to the Attorney

It would be good to talk to your attorney, to ask questions:

- What is the process for this particular crime, for this particular court?

- When do they need to go to court?

- If they are going to court, are they going to be sentenced?

- What will happen with their bills and accounts if they are convicted?

My brother had moved away before the court hearing. We didn't have a lot of information about his finances.

Also, the attorney can let you know if it would make sense for family members or others to testify in defense of your loved one. If it is, and you bring people with you to talk, the attorney can prepare them. There are a lot of things the attorney can do to help you prepare for the sentencing or the trial.

If the attorney hasn't provided this information, you can reach out to them and ask what you can do to prepare for court, what the sentence might be, and how long the process will take.

After the Guilty Verdict

There wasn't much we could do. My brother became a ward of the state. We had no rights, and we didn't know what to do. There was nobody to tell us what to do. The attorney told us to go home. We were in shock; we were like zombies. We went home, not realizing we were now a prison family.

We had yet to learn when a loved one is taken into the system, they are a ward of the prison, and from that point forward:

Visiting your loved one is a privilege.

It depends on which law they broke and who is prosecuting if they become a ward of your state or the federal government. Once your loved one is taken away, you have no legal rights to know where your loved one is and what is happening.

In preparation, you can also secure documents, such as a power of attorney. You can have legal documents set up to find out how your loved one is doing once they are processed to the facility they will be spending time in.

When my brother was taken away, we didn't have any of his information. I have spoken with people who have prepared finances prior to going to court. They have chosen someone to take care of business. My brother didn't do any of that. My parents were able to gain entrance into his apartment, and we were able to remove his belongings.

We donated his clothes and a lot of his stuff. His car was repossessed. He had some credit card debt. They called me, and I told them he was in prison so there was nothing I could do. He was no longer a part of society. Everything he owned was gone. He was locked up for life. It's not that he wasn't a person, but he didn't exist in our society anymore.

All his stuff—everything—was wiped out.

If your loved one is found innocent or guilty, they are taken back to the jail for processing. If found not guilty, you will be able to pick your loved one up at the jail, but be patient; it could take all day or even overnight.

If your loved one is found guilty, find out what the visitation rules are so you can see them while they are still at that jail. Once they are taken from the jail to the processing or evaluation facility, you will have little to no contact with them. This is where they'll be evaluated to determine which facility they'll be sent to.

Fill out all the visitation paperwork as soon as possible so that when you find out where they are going to start serving their sentence, you're already in the system and maybe even approved for visitation.

Important Points

RECAP: Get as much information as possible from your loved one prior to the trial to ensure everything can be managed and people notified in case they are taken into custody.

Here is a checklist of some information and items you need to obtain from your loved one:

- Legal documents
- Keys
- ID
- Bills and financial statements
- Children and their care
- Animals and their care
- Work contacts
- Friends list
- Vehicles and insurance
- Any other matters that need to be addressed

1. Once you've collected all the information from your loved one, ensure they take vital

items with them when they go to court, such as eyeglasses.

2. Additionally, get as much information as possible from the attorney.

3. This is another point at which you need to prepare yourself to see your loved one in a jumpsuit and possibly shackled from their ankles to hands. You may not be able to talk to them; you may not be able to see them again before they're taken away. They may not look at you.

4. Remember to fill out any forms for visitation, put money on your loved one's account, and take care of other needs as required by the facility.

Chapter Three

Visitation

VISIT PREPARATION

When someone is incarcerated and you haven't been through it before, it's difficult to know what to do. It's not intuitive. This chapter provides information on what to do when somebody is sentenced.

Information on Visitation

When my brother was taken into custody, we didn't have any communication with him for over a month. We didn't know who to talk to, and we couldn't visit him. We learned he was taken to a processing facility after he was sentenced and assigned an inmate number. This is where they evaluate inmates; it's called the *fish tank*. They do a physical and psychological evaluation to determine which prison they will be sent to, based on their sentence and their crime.

I can't explain the feeling of not knowing what was going on at the time. Back then, I was too ashamed to talk to anybody. I couldn't pick up the phone to ask because it was so surreal, having him incarcerated, not knowing what to do, and being too ashamed to talk to anyone. This is when my self-imposed prison sentence started; I started serving his sentence with him.

I finally received a letter from him, containing instructions on what we were supposed to do. Back then, before the days of the internet, we had to wait for him to mail us the information on forms and what we had to do. Now, you can go online.

Many facilities will have visitation instructions and the forms to fill out or download online. For other facilities, you need to wait for your loved one to send you the forms. You can even call the facility. However, be patient—it may take a while to get in touch with someone who will provide you the information you need.

Once you are approved for visitation, there will be certain days and times you can visit.

Filling Out the Paperwork

Once I received the application forms, I made copies for my parents. We filled them out and submitted them. We had to send them to a certain address in the prison system. It took about a month before we were approved to visit him. During that time, he was transported to his first prison. This would be the first of at least five prisons he went to. Some people reside in more prisons than that. For my brother, he was often moved for safety reasons because he had problems with another inmate or a medical issue.

I later learned he was on suicide watch for the first couple of days he was there. It is common for anyone who is given a life sentence. They put him in a bare room so he wouldn't hurt himself. I don't know if he received any psychological help while he was there; he never spoke about it. I learned from talking to and interviewing others that he was probably not provided the initial care he needed. I can't imagine what it's like to go from being a free man with all his rights and freedoms to having little to no hope of being free again.

The one thing we learned on the application form is *every field needs to be filled out.* I was talking to a friend who told me her approval was delayed. She was waiting and waiting, and she finally called. They said it wasn't approved, and she asked why. There was a blank field. She left her middle name blank because she doesn't have one. They actually told her she had to put *NMN* in there for no middle name. She had to fill out the form again and resubmit it. She had to wait another three weeks before it was approved.

So for her, it was a while before she got to see her daughter.

It's important you fill out every field on the form.

Logistics

Often when someone is arrested, they are brought to a local jail. In our case, the jail was an hour away. In order to see my brother, we had to drive there. Then he was moved to the processing facility three hours away, so it was more difficult to see him. Then, he was moved to another facility four hours away.

When he was at the facility three hours away, luckily for us, the visiting hours were Saturday and Sunday from 9 to 3. I didn't have to take time off work. I could drive up on Saturday morning, spend the night, and leave Sunday after our visit. But not all places are like that. You need to know the days and times of the visitation hours.

My brother was moved to many facilities during the time he was incarcerated. Nobody from the prison calls you when your loved one is moved. I typically found out when I received a collect call from my brother, telling me where they'd moved him. I didn't have to fill out another visitation form, but I did need to know the visitations process and hours of the new facility. You never know where your loved one is going to be moved to.

If your loved one is in a federal prison, that is another story because not every state has federal prisons. If they do, they are usually in specified places in the state that might not be near where you live.

When he was moved the second and third times, I had moved out of state and had to fly in to see him. I not only had to make time to visit him, but I also had to figure out when I was going to visit him, where I was going to stay, and my budget. It would cost me over $500 to visit him because I had to pay for airfare, a rental car, and a hotel. I'd have to take Friday off to travel so I could visit on Saturday and Sunday. If I couldn't find a flight home on Sunday, I'd have to leave Monday and take another day off work.

If the visiting days were during the week, then I would have taken additional time off work and probably run out of vacation time. There is a lot of planning that goes into a visit.

There is also the emotional preparation.

Can you really prepare for that?

You never know what you're going to encounter. Knowing what a visit is like can help you prepare. The visits do get easier, but it's never easy.

THE PHYSICAL VISIT

You're going to see someone you love who is locked up, who is in prison, whose rights have been taken away for whatever reason. You know their life is very different from yours. They don't have the freedoms you have. This section talks about visitation to help you prepare for it.

Visiting a prison is not like going through security at an airport or other places where police and guards pat you down to make sure you are not carrying anything. It's a lot more traumatic and intrusive.

It's not only the physical process of being patted down, it's also being looked at like you could have done something wrong. That's the emotional part, the feeling you get.

What to Bring

Once we were approved, my parents and I picked a day to go visit my brother. Of all the days we picked, it happened to be Valentine's Day. It was on a Saturday. That's not why we picked it, but that seemed like a convenient day, the first day we could all be there. The visiting hours started at 9:00 a.m., so we arrived at 8:00.

When we got there, there was a line across the street from the entrance. It was a chilly February morning.

My mother has never really been in good health, so luckily there was a bench, and she sat there. We did chat with some other people. People got there at 7:30 in the morning to be first. I definitely remembered that for future visits.

Once we got to the front of the line, they called our names. We had to be processed because it was our first visit.

For our first visit, we were told:

1. Know your loved one's inmate number

2. Bring an ID, one car key, and a clear plastic bag to hold everything.

3. We could bring fifty dollars in coins and small bills for the vending machines.

4. We could buy food if we were going to be there several hours. (It's also a treat for your loved one.)

5. My mother had to bring her medication in the the pharmacy bottle with the label. She could only bring the number of pills she would need during the visit.

Everything else, we had to leave in the car. This was what we could bring into the facility we were visiting.

The First and Subsequent Visits

To process us for the first visit, they scanned our fingerprints on a scanning machine. They would use our fingerprints to verify our identity for each visit. They also gave us a card with a number on it so in the future we didn't have to bring our ID; we simply had to know the number.

Once we were processed, we were able to go to a waiting area. We had to wait for the officer to call our names. Once they called our names, we walked through a metal detector. We were each taken into a room separately and patted down, front and back, by a guard of the same gender.

We had to take our shoes off. They looked inside the shoe to make sure there was nothing in the shoe or on the bottom of the shoe. They patted down the backs of our feet. Women had to pull their bras out to make sure they were not hiding anything in them. The guard also ran her hand through my hair to make sure there was nothing in my hair.

One note for women: Do not wear a bra with an underwire because it can set off the metal detector and your visit could be denied.

Once we were searched, I met my parents in the hallway, and we were escorted into the visiting area. We had to wait for guards to signal the other guards to open the door. We heard a loud click, and the door opened. We walked through the door, and there was a loud clank. We were now locked into the visiting area. The guards escorted us to a table and then left.

My parents and I sat there and looked at each other. There was a table with another two guards sitting there. Finally, the back door opened up, a different door from the one we came in, and my brother walked in.

It was so awkward. He walked over to the table. We hugged him, and he sat down. We were allowed to have one hug when he came out and one hug when he left. This is a pretty standard rule. I don't remember what we said, but it was hard to sit there without bawling.

There were other families sitting there, laughing and playing games. The facility made playing cards available. There were some other games and books for the kids. Children were allowed to sit on their parents' laps and run around. If they got too rowdy, the guards would stop them.

All I could think on this first visit was: *How could people be laughing in such a horrible place?*

We went to the vending machine to purchase some food, but there wasn't a lot left. We noticed people had piled food on their tables. As soon as I arrived in subsequent visits, I purchased food. We were lucky when the commissary opened; they had food there that we could order. The vending machine had sandwiches and hamburgers; it wasn't the best food, but it was a treat, especially for my brother.

While we were waiting to come in, my mother was assigned a locker for her pills. When it was time for her to take her pills, she told the guard, and he escorted her out so she could take her them.

My parents were so drawn out, so sad and forlorn. It was so heartbreaking, watching them look at their son. He came out wearing his blue prison uniform, and the shoes were plastic. He had taped glasses. When he had been taken into custody, he didn't have his glasses with him. Because he didn't have them with him, he had to find glasses while he was there. Luckily, he managed to get a pair, but they were old and taped.

Reminder: If your loved one uses glasses, tell them to wear them on the day of sentencing.

After sitting a while, we decided to go outside to the designated area. On that day, there was a wedding going on. It was Valentine's Day. To us at that time, it was so unbelievable. Why would anyone want to get married in prison? We couldn't understand it. But I know differently now. We stop seeing people in prison as having feelings. They are still human beings who experience emotions, such as love. People in love get married, despite the circumstances. That first day, it was mind-boggling.

That visit on Saturday was the last visit for my parents. They never saw my brother again. It was too emotional for my mother. She had a heart condition. I think my dad used it as an excuse; it was too painful to see his son in prison. Shortly after the visit, he disowned my brother. He didn't want anything to do with him. He removed him from his will.

My father never forgave my brother, but I think he harbored his own guilt that there was something he might have done, maybe when my brother was younger, to help him.

Was there anything that could have been done to change the situation? Guilty or not, my brother was serving a life sentence. I visited him as much as I could over the fifteen years he was incarcerated.

He served his life sentence. He died in prison in 2012.

WHAT WE LEARNED

There are certain rules you need to know when you visit a prison.

Read the rules because if you don't follow them, you can be:

1. Turned away from the visit
2. Sent away during the visit
3. Arrested, if you are actually doing something illegal
4. Denied future visits

You need to realize that once you're there, the prison officers have full rights. They can search you; they can search your car. When you are visiting a prison, even though you are a free person, you must abide by their rules. You need to respect the guards because they have all the authority.

It's good to know what you can bring and how to act.

What to Bring

It's important to know what to bring when visiting. *Remember my earlier point: visiting a loved one in prison is not a right, it's a privilege.* If you are wearing the wrong clothes, wrong shoes, the wrong color, or bring something in that could be considered contraband, they can deny your visit. When I was spending over $500 to visit my brother, the last thing I wanted was not be able to see him. That only happened once in the fifteen years I visited him.

You must know the rules. Your loved one can send them to you. My brother had sent me the rules about what I could wear and bring. Now, you can find it online. The inmates wore blue at my brother's facility. Visitors could not wear blue. They didn't want visitors to look like inmates.

I always wore short-sleeved or long-sleeved shirts because a tank top or a sleeveless top could be construed as showing too much skin. It's usually up to the guards. You can't wear short-shorts or skirts; they have to be three inches above the knee. I usually wore pants or capris and closed-toed shoes. They sometimes allowed sandals, and sometimes they wouldn't. It's really up to the guards as to what you can wear.

I could bring a clear plastic bag to hold my items, so they were visible to the guards. I could bring a closed bag of tissues, a small brush, a car key, small bills, and coins. I could wear my prescription glasses. That is basically what I walked in with.

I always carried an extra pair of clothes in the car. If I was wearing something that a guard deemed inappropriate, I could go back to the car and put something else on. One time, there was a woman wearing shorts, and they wouldn't let her in because her shorts were too short. I had pants I could lend her. Other people bring extra clothes too.

The sign-ups for games and playing cards are with the guard, and I learned to sign up as soon as I arrived because there were only a few decks of cards and games; they went fast. In subsequent visits, I was able to have a photo taken of my brother and me. One of the inmates is provided a Polaroid camera — the ones that click and print, nothing high-tech here — and charges a few dollars to take your photo with your loved one. Granted, the inmate does not get the money. Everything goes into the inmate fund or however they deem it to be used at the facility.

What to Talk About and How to Act

Have respect for the guards. Bite your tongue, if you need to. They are the authority, so they can decide if you can come in and visit or not. When I first arrived to see my brother, I was allowed to give him a hug. When I left, I could give him a hug. For my brother and me, that was fine.

When a husband or wife comes in to see their spouse, they aren't allowed a lingering embrace. I've heard guards tell people, "That's enough." Maybe visitors could give a little kiss on the lips, but no intimacy is allowed when a couple is visiting.

Young children could sit on their parents' laps. It's all up to the discretion of the guards how much contact parents can have with their children. I saw many families enjoying games during a nice visit. The first time I visited, it was really tough and I couldn't understand it. In subsequent visits, I recognized family time is so important, not just for the children, but also for the inmate. Many inmates would be going home in time, and keeping the family ties was important.

One of the hardest parts when visiting, at this facility especially, was that I wasn't allowed to talk to anyone in the visiting area. If there was another person at the table next to me, I couldn't talk to them. I couldn't talk to other inmates. The only people I could talk to were my brother and anyone who came with me to visit him.

This is another reason the guards might tell someone to leave: if they are breaking the *no talking* rule. When all of us were waiting in lines in the morning to be processed, we could talk to each other. That's when I learned about getting there early and buying food; those are things other people — who had been visiting there longer than me — shared with me.

Most fellow visitors were very helpful. Once we were inside, we looked at each other and didn't say a word. Maybe at the vending machine, you'd say *Hi*. But sitting at the tables, we could only talk to the people we came with and our loved one.

Being there several hours, I had to use the restroom. I'd have to ask the guard to unlock it for me. Only one person was allowed in there at a time. It was a big ordeal. My brother would rarely go to the restroom when we were visiting, which I think must have been difficult because I'd be there several hours.

To use the restroom, inmates had to exit through the door where they had entered. My understanding was they were allowed to use the restroom, but before they came back in, they had to be strip-searched. It was a big ordeal, and it took a chunk of time from the visit if they did have to go to the restroom. It's not as easy for them to *go* as it is for you.

What Can Happen During a Visit

During our first visit, the guard announced, "Count." All the inmates stood and lined up against the perimeter of the wall. *What was going on?* Nobody told us about this counting procedure.

They do the count several times during the day at the prison to make sure all the inmates are present. I became used to this count in subsequent visits. Sometimes they would line up in different places. Sometimes the guards would make them go outside to line up. It all depended on the guards.

The visiting room was like a high school cafeteria with long tables. Visitors may find themselves sitting with another family at the same table, but again, they couldn't talk to each other.

If something troublesome happens in the prison, they can put the prison in **lockdown**. There is a myriad of reasons why they lock down a prison—finding contraband, or a fight. During lockdown, no one can visit.

You can't call the prison before you visit to ask if they are in lockdown. When you show up, they will simply tell you you can't visit. This luckily only happened to me one time on a Saturday when I flew out, but I visited him on a Sunday. In fifteen years, that only happened once.

Be courteous to the guards. If you're smart with them, if you're rude to them, if you don't listen to them— they can revoke your visit. Remember the big picture; they're people too. They have good days and bad days. Treat them with respect. It doesn't guarantee you will be treated with respect, but in situations like this, you need to swallow your pride to make sure you can spend time with your loved one.

When I visited my brother, it was really tough. I tried to hold it together when I was with him. I rarely ever cried in front of him. I'd be fine on Saturday because I was planning on seeing him on Sunday. But on Sunday, I'd hold it together until I left. When I walked out on Sundays, I couldn't hold it in anymore. It was tough and emotional.

I was mostly alone. Because my parents didn't go after the first visit, it was just me for ten years. Then, my husband went with me.

One time as I was leaving, the guard looked at me and said, "Why are you crying?"

I looked at her like, *Really?* I looked at her and left. It's something no one understands if they haven't been through it.

There are female guards in the male prison and male guards in the female prison. Don't be surprised when you see them.

Different people have different routines to help them prepare for their visit. Some people are excited to see their loved ones. But there is also that trepidation, that fear, that guilt because sometimes people are treated as if they did something wrong.

You need to remember that you didn't do anything wrong. You are going to see your loved one. Just remember that.

Important Points for Visitation

RECAP:

1. Fill out any forms (e.g., for visitation, putting money on your loved one's account).

2. Read the visitation regulations (know what you can bring and wear).

3. You can bring the allowable amount of money, a brush or comb, one key, and a sealed package of tissues in a clear bag. (Make sure to read the rules for the facility you are visiting on what you can bring.) You may try to not cry while you're there, but you may need the tissues when you leave (also helpful if there's no toilet paper).

4. Wear conservative clothes. Interpretation of the rules is up to the guards, and they can deny your visit if your clothes are deemed inappropriate. What's appropriate one week may not be deemed appropriate the following week. If you are driving, always carry extra clothes and shoes in your car in case you need to change.

5. Remember your car is subject to search. Do not have anything in your car that can be construed as contraband (know the rules).

6. Know the visitation days and hours, and arrive as early as they allow.

7. If you're going to buy food during your visit, purchase what you want as soon as you arrive. The vending machines run out of food quickly.

8. Create a schedule and a budget for your visit.

9. Treat guards with respect (they can deny your visit).

10. Understand count and lockdown. Count can occur while you are sitting there with your loved one and when the guard calls "count," all the inmates have to line up in a designated area. Once the guard(s) complete counting the inmates, your loved one will be allowed to return to you. Lockdown is when something occurs within the prison, and nobody is allowed in to visit.

11. Sign up right away for games and photos.

Chapter Four

Stories

MY BROTHER DIED IN PRISON

The last thing anybody thinks about is being incarcerated and possibly being ill or dying in prison. That is the last place anybody wants to be sick or spend their last days, taking their last breath. However, it does happen. People do die in prison, and it can happen to your loved one. If it does, here is the information you need to know.

Terminal Illnesses

There are many illnesses and injuries that can happen to someone who is incarcerated that can cause them to pass away. In my brother's case, he had hepatitis C. Hepatitis C is a liver disease that can be in somebody's system for many, many years — up to thirty. According to the CDC, one in three people who are incarcerated have hepatitis C, a number that has grown over the years.[1]

When my brother told me he had hepatitis C, he had no signs. He was healthy. The internet wasn't prevalent back then. I didn't do any research on it because I didn't know it was a terminal illness. It wasn't until 2012, fifteen years after he was incarcerated, that I went to visit him and saw what hepatitis C was.

I discovered it was terminal one day when my husband and I visited him. We were sitting there in the visiting room waiting for him. We hadn't seen him for several months because of other life circumstances.

My brother was wheeled in by an officer. We didn't even know he needed a wheelchair and oxygen. They wheeled him up to the table. All I could do was hold back my tears. I had no idea how sick he was. I had no idea hepatitis C was going to take his life. He was jaundiced. His skin was an orange color and all shriveled up. He looked like an old man; he looked like Yoda from *Star Wars*.

His stomach was protruding because hepatitis C is a liver disease, and the liver expands, becoming bloated and inflamed. He was weak; he didn't have

1 "Hepatitis C & Incarceration." *Centers for Disease Control*, publication No. 21-1306. October 2013. cdc.gov/hepatitis/hcv/pdfs/hepcincarcerationfactsheet.pdf

a lot of energy. We spent a little bit of time with him, only a couple hours. It was too much for him; the visit wore him out.

We did talk about his final wishes as he was very ill. We found out what he wanted us to do when he passed. We already knew he wanted to be cremated. He told us to do whatever we wanted with the ashes. When we left, we wanted to see him again.

Facilities don't call you and tell you your loved one is ill. We didn't know he was sick until we saw him. We spoke to the assistant warden, and he worked with us to plan to visit my brother the following week in the infirmary.

We were going to come back, but he didn't make it. We saw him on Saturday. We were coming back the following weekend, but he passed on Tuesday.

Power of Attorney

When my brother was first incarcerated, he sent me information on how to file for power of attorney. He had gotten the forms and sent them to me to fill out; I completed them and sent them back. During the time he was incarcerated, I could call and speak to his caseworker.

When someone is incarcerated, it's really important that you have this information. Otherwise, you have no right to receive any information about their health, how they're doing, or if there are any updates in that area. Make sure you know what legal documents are required and if and when they need to be renewed.

Having power of attorney doesn't mean you will have special access to your loved one when they are in solitary or in lockdown, or if there are any infractions. All those rules are still the same. It also doesn't mean anyone will call you when your loved one has an issue or health problem at the prison.

In this case, I could call and receive information on his health. If I had known he was so sick prior to our visit, I could've called to get more information. If he had shared his condition with me, I could have monitored the situation and made sure he was getting the medicine and medical attention he needed. He didn't tell me because he didn't want me to worry.

If Your Loved One Passes

Each prison is different. In my case, because I had been in touch with the assistant warden, he called me the Tuesday after the visit. He told me that my brother had passed peacefully. He was very compassionate. We discussed the options. The state would cremate him, which was what I had discussed with my brother.

You can make arrangements if you want to have a burial. These are things you can find out from the prison. They told us where he was going to be cremated. We picked up the ashes. We had permission to sprinkle them over a lake. We did that with some friends. We had a little memorial, and we each had a rose. We sprinkled the ashes and put the roses into the water. It was a good ceremony, and I think that's what he would have wanted me to do.

SELECTED STORIES

Over the years, I have spoken to a lot of people whose loved ones have addictions. It's often because of these addictions they are incarcerated. It's really heartbreaking for the parents of the loved ones to find out their children have been incarcerated. Often, family members don't know their loved one had an addiction to drugs or alcohol.

This section discusses what can happen in prison, what brings people into prison, and how it affects the family. Drug addiction and alcoholism are really big factors, especially for the families who are dealing with loved ones cycling in and out of prison for many years because of their addictions.

I have a couple of stories to share.

Drug Addiction: Heather's Story

Heather's son was arrested because of something he did while he under the influence of drugs. Heather wasn't aware her son had a drug problem. He wasn't living at home. He was sentenced when he was nineteen years old. He was barely a man, and he served ten years of his sentence. *Ten years*. During the whole time he was incarcerated, her family visited, they emailed, they spoke to him on the phone, they contacted him, and they supported him. She attended Narcotics Anonymous — meetings for families, not the person who has the addiction. In those ten years, she supported him, and she supported herself.

He was twenty-nine when he came out. He told her when the release date was and where to pick him up. She proceeded to the meeting place and waited for three hours for the white, unmarked van to show up.

Finally, the white van arrived. Two men got out, and one was her son. She said, "I can't even describe that feeling. Just running up to him and giving him a hug and knowing he was a free person."

She couldn't explain how she felt now that her son was out of prison. She had been serving a sentence with him. A lot of people don't realize that. When you have an incarcerated loved one, you are serving a sentence with them. So, she was freed also. That first morning, they went to breakfast as a free family.

When somebody comes out of prison, they could be wearing prison-issued clothes. Her son was wearing blue jeans and a blue shirt. Heather brought him a shirt. I hear this a lot: when people come out of prison, having new clothes there so they can change out of the clothes they have been wearing for years is so freeing for them. He changed, and they went to breakfast. He got his biscuits and gravy, and he was so happy.

After he was out, he did well for a while. After being in prison for ten years, he suffered from PTSD. He did resort back to drugs. His family got him into a drug program. He did well for a while, but the PTSD set in. They really couldn't do anything. He had this addiction. No matter how hard they tried to fight it, he couldn't fight it. He had another encounter, so he is currently in prison.

Heather said, "Who could've thought someone could have PTSD from being in prison?"

It's real. She tried to get him help, but it progressed to the point where he wouldn't listen. She couldn't help him anymore. It's tough love. She had to step back. She is still supporting him. The family is still supporting him. But he is back in prison.

Parents and Children: Esther and Dolores

Dolores' mother, Esther, said, "We made a decision not to hire an attorney. Our daughter was upset, but we were sticking to the tough love decision we made before the accident. No more enabling. We were drained mentally, physically, and financially."

Their daughter was assigned a public defender who Esther had confidence in. However, before the trial, a different public defender was assigned. This new attorney seemed inexperienced and folded during the trial, in Esther's opinion. They went to court four or five times.

Dolores was an alcoholic. Her mother knew it. The family had done everything they could, but Dolores was no longer living at home. She was an adult. She went on a driving spree when she was intoxicated, had an accident, and killed someone. Her mother Esther received that call.

Dolores said, "Mom, I killed someone."

Esther was in shock at this time because Dolores was supposed to be in a rehabilitation facility. Somehow, Dolores had signed herself out, found some alcohol, and went on a spree. Unfortunately, it ended fatally.

There were months of trials until she was sentenced. For Esther's family, it was especially difficult because several family members were in law enforcement. If somebody in your family is in law enforcement, it will be even more difficult for them because there is nothing they can do.

At the sentencing, Esther said it was difficult because the victim's family was in the room too. After her daughter was sentenced, Esther did go over to the family, and she gave her condolences to them. She felt horrible for what her daughter had done. One of the family members hugged her. Esther said she couldn't believe the strength of the victim's family. She knew they were forgiving people.

For months after the sentencing, it was Esther who suffered from PTSD.

Would you think someone on the outside would be affected?

As time went on, she felt better, but the pain was always working on her—that deep pain. She didn't cause it, but her daughter did. She never thought Dolores would live with her and her husband again. They were elderly, getting up there in age. When Dolores was released, several people spoke to Esther so she agreed Dolores could be paroled at home. She believed Dolores deserved another chance.

Right now, life does look promising. Dolores is home, doing well. But she will never forget the needless pain caused to another family.

NOTE: PTSD is not discussed in this book; however, upon the inmate's release, it can be experienced by them as well as by family members.

Coming Home

Calvin's son was not living with him at the time; he was only seventeen years old. Calvin found out on the news his son was incarcerated. He went through the whole ordeal of people knowing his son was incarcerated because it was on the news.

What would you do?

He couldn't hide from it. The trial was publicized, and his son was found guilty of the crime. Because the son was young, he was able to be in the youthful offenders' program. He felt a little better because his son would be with younger people. Calvin was still affected. The first time he pulled into the parking lot to visit his son, he felt physically ill, like someone kicked him in the stomach. It did get easier. Luckily, his mother helped Calvin get through it. He kept a journal, and that helped.

When his son was released, he had served only five years. He was still young. As far as Calvin can tell, his son has kept clean for the five years he has been out. He is going to his meetings, and it's good to have his son back home.

The important thing is to find support for the person who has the addiction. It's up to that person to take the necessary steps to heal. Some people can be rehabilitated, and for some, the addiction is too strong.

EMPATHY

I have learned over the years that if I had spoken about my struggles, if I had shared my story with people, I would have received compassion. I would have received the support I needed. Because of the guilt, shame, and depression I experienced being *on the outside* while my brother was incarcerated, I didn't talk about it. I didn't tell anyone. Because I didn't, I couldn't receive compassion from anybody.

Empathy is being with someone, being able to understand someone, being able to relate to something that someone else has gone through even if you haven't gone through it yourself. I experienced empathy when I joined the support group. That is where I could be with other people who understood what it was like to have a loved one incarcerated, to live on the outside, to visit prison, to experience the emotional and financial impacts of the experience on their lives.

I recommend joining a support group where you can receive the empathy you need when you are going through this process. When your loved one is incarcerated, when they go into solitary and you can't speak to them, these will be people you can talk to. That is why having a support group of people around you who have been through it is important.

You can also find safe people, people who you can trust and talk to. You may have a close friend, a relative, or a spiritual or religious leader who you can talk to.

You can have compassion for yourself too. I think it's really important that you take care of yourself, have compassion for yourself, and have compassion for your loved ones.

Showing compassion is the key to closing the empathy gap, so people are aware that incarceration affects more than the person who is incarcerated; it affects people on the outside too. When somebody does go to prison, they are not going by themselves. Their whole family is going. People who love them are going.

It's important that we talk about it, raise awareness, and show compassion to each other so people can receive the empathy they need while going through this experience. I think it will make prison families —

both the people who are incarcerated and who are outside — healthier so that when people do come out of prison, they are going into a healthy, compassionate environment. They can move on, find jobs, and become productive citizens of society.

Important Points

RECAP:

1. Ensure you have all legal documents needed: power of attorney along with medical and financial power, if allowed in your state, and a last will and testament. Make sure you know the rules for renewal of any legal documents so they don't expire.

2. Know who you can contact at prison: caseworker, warden, assistant warden, religious chaplains, and others. If you have the appropriate legal documents, then they can share information with you about your loved one.

3. Escalate concerns to the warden or assistant warden. They will talk to you.

4. If your loved one has a serious or terminal illness, establish a contact at the infirmary to talk to about your loved one's condition.

Follow up frequently to ensure they are receiving the care needed.

5. Establish boundaries for yourself and find safe people to talk to.

Chapter Five

Chapter Five

Healthy You—A Call to Action

SEEKING INFORMATION

When you are on the outside and your loved one is taken into the prison system, you need to know:

- What information you need
- Where to get the information
- How to use it
- How to take care of yourself and your family

If there are experiences you haven't lived through, if you have never been through the process or known anyone who was arrested and taken into the prison system, you might not know what questions to ask or what to look for.

Calling the Facility

Your loved one has been arrested and taken to jail.

What do you do?

- You can call the jail for information about your loved one. You can ask what they were accused of and ask questions about visitation, such as: Can I come see my loved one? Your loved one might only be there for an hour, or you may be able to pick them up. Or, they might be in there for several days, waiting to appear in court. If they are in there for several days and you want to visit them, there are certain things you need to know (See Chapter 1). If your loved one has already been sentenced and is incarcerated, and you have questions, you can call the facility.

- Every inmate is assigned a correctional case manager (the titles may differ at facilities). Ask your loved one to let you know the name of their correctional case manager so you may call them. The case manager may not be allowed to share certain information with you unless you have legal documents, such as power of attorney, allowed in that jurisdiction. Your loved one can provide the appropriate legal forms to you. You will have to find a notary to sign them once you've completed them. But should you need to call the case manager or anyone else in the prison, with the proper documents, they may be able to share information with you. If you have a problem reaching the correctional case manager, you can call the warden or the assistant warden.

- A facility usually has a family services department that can provide you with information on processes and procedures. Know that you have every right to call the facility housing your loved one to get information. Depending on the information you are requesting, you may need a power of attorney or other legal documents.

You should determine when it is best to call the facility. If you call all the time, they may not pay attention to you when it's really serious. Know when to call and who to call.

A side note: when you are mailing legal documents, make sure that is written on the outside of the envelope. The officers are not allowed to open legal documents.

Online Resources

Now, you might be wondering how and where to find the contact information for the people I just mentioned. Your loved ones should be able to provide you with a lot of this information. When they are going through processing, they are provided with information they can then provide to you.

The best thing you can do is go online to the website of the facility where your loved one is being held. These websites usually provide information on visitation along with the visitation application. You should fill out that application as soon as possible.

These websites also typically provide information on how to send money, how to correspond with your loved one—sending letters, emails, texting—and anything that is available and allowed at that particular facility. A lot of websites have information for family services and the contact information for the warden and other key officials. Look for a directory of phone numbers.

A lot of Department of Corrections' websites will have a copy of the inmates' handbook. This contains the information provided to your loved one when they are incarcerated. We are also seeing more and more websites with family and visitation handbooks, which include all the rules about what to wear, when to visit, what color to wear, what to bring, how to handle medicine or medical needs, and visits by children.

Again, remember that even though you know your loved one is in there and you think you can visit them: visitation is a privilege, not a right.

Attorneys and the Court

After your loved one is incarcerated, what can they do?

They still have the right to use the court system to file motions and appeals. Unfortunately, some inmates do not have the legal acumen to file these themselves. There are typically law libraries in the prisons so they can solicit information on how to file these motions and appeals.

If you have the means, it's better to work with and hire an attorney to file them. Chances are that even though a person may have been sentenced, there is something the attorney can help them with. I'm not a lawyer. I do know my brother filed these by himself. He filed them until he couldn't file them anymore, and he had nothing else to do. Make sure to talk to your loved ones about how to file motions and appeals, and secure legal assistance so they can do it right.

When your loved one is going through the trial process, there may not be a lot of information available to you. You need to request information from your attorney or public defender about the process and what you can do while your loved one is going through the trial. You will need your loved one's permission for the attorney to share information with you.

FINDING SUPPORT

The most important thing you can do while your loved one is serving time is to keep yourself healthy because they will hopefully be coming out someday. You want to be there for them, and you want to be healthy so you can support them. When they come out, they will have been through a traumatic experience. Keep yourself healthy so you may come up with a plan and provide support for your loved one when they come back home.

It's important to keep the prison family healthy, and that starts with you.

Professional Help

There is no shame in seeking professional help, in seeing a therapist to help with whatever you're going through while your loved one is behind bars. You're on the outside. It's normal to feel guilty, especially if you are having a good time and enjoying your life. You may suddenly find yourself thinking of your loved one sitting behind bars and become sad and feel guilty because you're out enjoying life and they're not. A therapist can help you with depression and setting boundaries in dealing with the situation.

They can help you with the loss. Losing someone is losing someone; it doesn't matter if it's a death, an addiction, or incarceration. The feelings of loss are similar to losing someone to death. You will miss them because they are not in your life anymore. You won't see them on a daily basis. Yes, you can talk to them. You can visit them. But for all intents and purposes, they're gone — whether it's for six months, six years, or sixteen years.

You can feel the same emotions as if they have passed away.

Some emotions you might feel are:

- *Depression*: At the loss of their presence in your life or when you go to visit them

- *Shock*: At them being taken away or for what they are accused of

- *Anger*: For what they were accused of doing, for the situation, or because they are in prison. Never speak to your loved one or anyone at the prison when you are angry. A good exercise is to write your feelings on a piece of paper and then tear it up.

- *Guilt*: For enjoying your life while they are in prison or when wondering if there was anything you could have done to help them or change the situation

A therapist can help you to acceptance. Accepting the situation is living your life.

Support Groups

Any time we go through a difficult time, it helps to be around people who have had similar experiences. Look for support groups in your area. There are also support groups online. With over six million people in the prison system, there are millions of people on the outside who are affected. You should be able to find people who have gone through this and are supporting each other.

If you can't find a support group in your area or online, start thinking about creating your own support group. There are probably people in your community who could use it, and you can help each other. Sometimes the best healing occurs by helping and talking to others.

I found a local support group that helped me not feel so alone. They also gave me suggestions on how to deal with challenges I was having with my brother, such as not feeling like a victim or like I did something wrong when I visited prison and talked to the guards.

It was always a scary experience for me. Being around other people in the support group helped me deal better with my situation, and I think it can help you.

Talking to Friends

Don't leave your friends out. Give them a chance to support you. If they don't know what you're going through, they can't help you. But also, you need to use your judgment about who to talk to. Consider friends who have lived through trauma so they can empathize with you. Make sure you talk to safe friends, people who have been with you, people who you know really well. Test the waters. Talk to one person and see how it goes. Take it from there. You may be amazed by what you find out when you start talking to people.

When I started talking about my brother's incarceration, I learned a friend I had known fifteen years had a daughter who was incarcerated. She didn't talk about it either. Talk about it, but make sure it's in a safe place with safe people.

A BALANCED LIFE

The only way to stay healthy emotionally and physically while your loved one is incarcerated is to take care of yourself. You do that by making sure you balance your life between your work, your friends and family, and things you do on the outside with what you give to your loved one who is incarcerated: how often you visit them, how you support them. These boundaries enable you to live a balanced life.

Setting Boundaries

Setting boundaries is important for you, for the people around you, for the groups you've joined, and especially for your loved ones. This is another element of how to keep yourself healthy. I keep repeating that so you can be there for your loved ones. When you are going through the process of shock, anger, guilt, and depression, you may not be in a position to make really smart decisions. A counselor or therapist and a good friend can help you set boundaries and make good decisions. They can help you determine what to look for when you are talking to people, who you should talk to, and how they can help keep you in safe situations.

Have you ever met somebody, and they told you their whole life story in the first five minutes after you met them?

Did you ever wonder why they told you all this? Did you care?

You might have listened to be courteous. Remember this experience when you tell someone about how your loved one's incarceration is affecting you. Make sure to set boundaries so you are not always talking about it. You don't want people to think: *she is going to talk about that again.*

You need to decide when to talk about it and who to talk to. Some people just won't care about your situation, and you need to be open to that. Know your boundaries and how to protect yourself, but also give yourself the freedom to talk about it to the right people.

Set boundaries and expectations between your incarcerated loved one and yourself. Figure out how often to visit. Your loved one might want you to visit more often. They might want to talk to you on the phone more. But, their requests might not be right for you. You need to set boundaries around how often to visit, how often to talk to them, and how often to correspond. If writing and emailing every day works for you, great. But if you need a break and are unable to do it emotionally or financially, then set your boundaries. You need to determine what works for you and set those expectations with your loved one.

Emotional Balance

Having a loved one incarcerated can be an emotional rollercoaster. You never know what they are going to say to you. You don't know what has happened to them. You can't be there to protect them or help them because you are on the outside. You only know what they've told you; you only know their side. Sometimes, it is good to have a relationship with their correctional case worker or someone at the prison. My brother would call with *situations*. Sometimes, there was nothing I could do about it, and sometimes, I just didn't understand what was happening. I would get upset and the next time he might be okay. So, I learned to let him vent and just listen and not react.

You might be out with your friends or at work and see something that reminds you of your loved one. Then you become emotional. I used to run to the bathroom and cry in the stall, wipe my eyes, and splash water on my face before I walked out so nobody saw my emotions.

Was this healthy?

No. It wasn't healthy because I didn't talk about it back then. Now, if I experience emotions, I can talk about them. When it's new and raw, you might want to keep your emotions private. As time goes on, you can learn different techniques for sharing your experience with others.

If a friend sees someone who reminds them of their loved one in the hospital, they get a tear in their eye. We understand. We need to get to the point where we can express emotions about our loved one and share it with people so they understand.

If your emotions start running your life, a therapist can help you. You can learn techniques to deal with your emotions. It's a process.

You may want to try working out and/or meditating. Even deep breathing can help calm you down. In fact, take a few deep breaths before you speak to your loved one. They'll feel your calmness and it will help them calm down, too.

Financial Smarts

Having a loved one in the prison system is not cheap. It's not. Depending on your means, you need to determine how much money you're going to put on your loved one's account when they are incarcerated. There are typically a couple of services — JPay, Western Union, and some others — that allow you to send money through third parties to your loved ones, and your loved one will then have an account to draw from.

What do they need money for?

Depending on whether they use a calling card or call you collect, you may need to put money on their account for a calling card. They may use a third-party system for sending or receiving emails.

They are furnished only basic toiletries. They might want to purchase additional toiletries, clothing — like socks or sweatshirts — paper, and writing utensils. In the commissary, they can purchase food. Sometimes, they can buy a TV, radio, player, classes, or music for a tablet.

Initially, you may provide money for your loved ones so they can be a little more comfortable while serving their sentence. The prison may be close to you. However, if your loved one is incarcerated for any length of time, chances are they will be moved. They could be moved several times, so they may move far away from you. You may need to budget for transportation.

Traveling involves answering several questions to determine expenses:

1) How are you going to get there?

   a) Are you going to drive?
   b) Are you going to take the bus?
   c) Are you going to fly?
   d) Will you need to rent a car?

2) Where are you going to stay? Do you need to reserve a hotel?

3) What food will you need?

4) Care for children and/or animals?

If you're going to visit them, do you want to bring money so that you and your loved one can purchase food and drinks during your visit? They usually have vending machines and a commissary. You might also want to purchase a photo of you and your loved one while you're there, as I described in Chapter Three.

You also need to consider time off work too. Each facility has different visiting days. I was lucky because visiting days were on Saturday and Sunday. He was far away, so I would fly out on Friday and fly home on Sunday. But in order to do this, I had to take time off work. If visiting hours are only during the week, I would have had to take more time off work, take a vacation, or take unpaid leave for those days.

If you have children or animals, you will need to set up care for them if the facility is not within driving distance or if you are not taking your children with you.

Set boundaries for yourself to keep your emotional well-being, your health, and your finances in balance as you traverse this alternate universe known as the prison system.

Take care of yourself by eating healthy, working out (even if it's just short walks), quiet time (meditation if you like), deep breaths and finding support with safe people. The healthier you are the better you'll be able to be there for yourself and your loved ones. You deserve to be happy.

Conclusion

I hope this book provides you with the information you need to navigate the process of having your loved one taken into the prison system:

- To help you find and speak with an attorney or public defender if that is the route your family takes

- To help you know what to expect on the inside, from the parking lot to the visiting area

- To help you prepare for your visits by knowing what to bring and what clothes to wear so you may share a good visit with your loved one

- To help you enjoy and experience a fulfilled life while your loved one is serving their term in prison

As you live through the whole process, keep a balanced life. Know that the healthier you are, the more support and help you provide to your loved one.

Most of all, I hope this book leaves you with the courage to speak about your experience because the more that people speak about it, the more other people will understand. The more people understand, the more likely we can affect change in the prison system.

I would like to know what helped you and what you have learned. The more information we share, the more we help others going through this. If we share this information, nobody feels alone, like they are going through it by themselves.

By telling your story, you free yourself and provide information to others.

Remember: know your boundaries and your safe people to talk to.

I'd also like you to share this book if it helps you. When you run across someone else who has a loved one who has been arrested and incarcerated, share this book with them. If you come across someone who has never known anyone incarcerated, who doesn't understand you or your situation, share this book with them. This book can help them understand or gain insight as to what it's like to have somebody taken into the prison system, what it's like for the family. Hopefully, they will then be open and share compassion instead of blaming the family for something out of their control.

In the end, no one has control over anyone else. We can influence, but we can't change our loved one's addiction. We can't change our loved one's problems.

We can't change the fact our loved one was hanging out with the wrong people or was in the wrong place at the right time.

I've learned to live for each day because you don't know what tomorrow has in store for you. Tomorrow could bring the greatest thing that's ever happened to you, or it could be the most traumatic thing. When you're with your loved ones, tell them you love them. Be with them. Be present. When someone is taken from you, your life changes. Whether it be prison, a terminal illness, an addiction, or whatever, cherish and live for today, and be prepared for tomorrow.

Finally, I'd like to leave you with one thought: *Be compassionate to each other.*

Next Steps

To contact Julia and find out more about her advocacy, about the effects of incarceration on your family and community, and for tips on how to handle these difficult situations, go to https://prisonthehiddensentence.com.

About the Author

Julia Lazareck is an advocate for change for family members whose loved ones are incarcerated. Her brother received a life sentence and served it when he died of hepatitis C while incarcerated.

Through her blog, podcast, publications, and presentations, Julia provides information on the prison family journey from arrest to re-entry. She shares her story and the stories of others to raise awareness and close the empathy gap concerning this difficult journey.

Not only does Julia provide information to families and work to educate communities, she also facilitates programs that share critical information about traversing the criminal justice system. In addition, she works with non-profits that offer support to the families and children of incarcerated parents.

When Julia is not advocating, she spends time with her wonderful husband of over twelve years. They live in a net-zero electric home and practice energy and environmental efficiency. Julia has been a professional project manager for over fifteen years.

Julia's goal is to make the world better for future generations by raising awareness and educating people so we can better understand and show compassion to each other.

Made in the USA
Monee, IL
01 April 2024

56163598R00066